Index

Index: 3/4/5
Copyright issue   6
Charities receiving donations   7/8
Acknowledgements   9
About 'Reflections'   10

Romance   11
Ode to My Lady   12
Valentine's Day   13
Sweetheart   14
Beloved   15

Remembrance: 16
Wootton Bassett - Thank You   17
Grieving   18
Conscientious Objectors   19
Be Not Alone   20
The Loss Felt   21

Making the best of it: 22
A Mind To Ponder   23/24
Tomorrow Waits   25
Homeless And On the Street   26/27
Darkness In Life   28
The Wheelchair   29

PTO

Index cont:

Prayers and Hymns   30

Do Not Forget	31
Boy In A Stable	32
Battle Hymn	33
Rejoice	34
Prayer—Church Re-opening	35

Christmas Poems: 36

Christmas Joy	37
A Baby Arrives At Christmas	38
Christmas Wish	39
Snowman III	40/41
Jesus's Birthday	42
Christmas	43

Animal Antics   44

The Fox Cubs	45
Little Thrush	46
The Mouse	47
The Music of The Birds	48
2 Cats & 1 Dog	49

Fun Time: 50

Ooh La La!	51
Puddings	52
Dad Your Parkinson's A Pain	53
A Good Nights Sleep	54
Laughing Child	55

Index cont:

Mobility   *56*

A Chariot   57

A Bike for A Girl   58

Motor Car   59

Our Journey   60

The Trip   61

Out and About   *62*

Bath   63

The Village   64

Corsham Town   65

Tranquil Place   66

Café Church   67

Finally: *68*

Stand Tall and Proud   69

A Friend   70

Love Is Yours   71

Our Journey   72

A Nation true   73

Reflections Around My Life

By J. A. Johnston

First Edition

A Jay Publisher Book: ISBN 978-0-9573877-0-6

Jay Publisher.

jaypublisher@gmx.com

Printed in Great Britain by
imprintdigital.net. Devon.

Charities to receive donations from sales:

It is the author's intention that the following four charities should benefit from the sale of this book:

Parkinson's UK – Malmesbury branch:

This charity is close to the authors heart: Sylvia and her committee are very active in ensuring the members get the best entertainment and outings possible. It is hoped that the sale of this book will, in some small way, ensure a continuation of finances.

Talking Newspapers – Chippenham:

The author finds this charity a very useful one for those of poor, failing or failed sight. The author also reads for this charity and is to make this book available on disc for those who would prefer a sound recording.

Friends of Bwindi:

This charity is run by friends of the author and supports a group of villagers who have been expelled from the Bwindi Rain forest. In being expelled these villagers lost their livelihood. Friends of Bwindi run three main projects: Bwindi Community Hospital, Stay Safe Children's Foundation, along side a HIV/Aids education program.

PTO

Corsham Churches Foodbank

The Churches of Corsham came together to form Corsham Churches Foodbank (CCFbnk) in summer of 2010. The idea being to provide food parcels for those in need. Since that time the CCFbnk has provided 496 meals for those in need—a very BIG THANK YOU—to all those donors from Corsham and the surrounding area.

John

Acknowledgements

Firstly to my beloved wife Val who spent a great deal of time and energy in persuading me to start writing again after many years, suggesting that I produce this book, editing some of the poems. God bless you Val.

I would also like to thank Jill Elliott for her encouragement and assistance in putting this book of poems together.

Also to Carol Kibble for her painting on:
'Wootten Bassett—Thank You'

Not forgetting Bryan and Jon, without whom I could not have published this book.

My sincere thanks to you all.

John

About 'Reflections'

I have lived a varied, enjoyable and sometimes downright stupid life.

As the past is left behind and I mature, I find myself reflecting on what I have experienced.

I discovered quite early on that I gained solace from writing my thoughts down.

As I developed and allowed others into my secret world of writing, it became apparent that others enjoyed, or at least took comfort from what I had written.

I have written many poems, songs, hymns and plays which cover a wide variety of events from sitting in the garden watching the wildlife and people, thinking of bereavement, romance, dark times, religion and many other subjects.

Thank you for taking the trouble to read this book.

John

Romance

Ode to My Lady: I wrote this as an ode to my wife—I did mean every word of it; really.

Valentine's Day: I do not need to say why I wrote it!

Sweetheart: I wrote this originally as a poem but my wife suggested I put a tune to it and turn it into a song. The tune used was composed by Phil Hall. It is now part of the repertoire of 'End of the Track' - a men's singing group in Chippenham, Wiltshire.

Beloved: This I wrote while thinking on how much I loved my wife and all that she had done for 'us'. It was also to actually tell her how much I loved her.

Romance:

Ode To My Lady

If truth be known, I fell for you
On that bright Easter Time,
When out we went, what a great day we spent
The children, you and I.

Like a pair of old slippers we were that day,
As we went on our way
Listened to music, played poo-sticks
On a bridge not far away.

With children's laughter I was blessed,
She encourages us in all that we do,
Even when all seems lost,
Her love is for ever strong.

Some diets she likes to stick
Loosing weight quite quick,
But the Chocolate, oh heck,
Her love is for ever strong.

Her emotions are batty,
Though sometimes quite scatty,
But she stands by me, when a need has been
Her love is for ever strong

But to end this ode,
To the lady I owe
All my love, to one
My love is ever so strong.

We ALL love you - so there!

©*J. A. Johnston*
October 2004

Romance:

Valentines Day

Valentines Day is especially for you to tell you that I love you true
But He from up above sent you to be the one I love.

This choice was made when you sent Him a list of a man just for you
I thought He'd short changed you by giving this worthless soul to you.

But you have made the best of life making you my wife
By taking me for life you've entertained much trouble and strife.

I am ever grateful to Him for lifting me from sin
Taking me out of life's bin freeing me up from sin.

Showing me the way to better things, making my soul a twin with you
Forever now I'll be with you, because I am in purest love with you.

So on Valentine's day just believe me when I say
I love you, not just this day but now and for always

Romance:

Sweetheart

My heart belongs to you sweetheart.
My heart will always be yours.
My heart is full of love for you.
Sweetheart, Sweetheart, Sweetheart.

Is your heart for me my love?
Is your heart forever mine?
Is your heart full of love for me?
Sweetheart, Sweetheart, Sweetheart.

With you by my side
I've a smile so wide
I could not be without you
Oh yes my love it's true.

Our hearts are forever entwined
My heart and your heart together
Our hearts are full of love for each other
Sweetheart, Sweetheart, Sweetheart.
Sweetheart, you're mine, Sweetheart.

©J. A. Johnston
25th April 2010

14

Romance :

Beloved

The depth of my love is immeasurable to me
As deep a rose red or as feelings can be.
Only she knows what she feels for me
My love is deeper than the deepest sea green.

The love that I have is shown not through wealth
But all that I can give; like my heart
Only she knows what I have for her
Is beyond her deepest or wildest of dreams.

She can but be herself for me, pure and clean
For herself I love her dearly
True friends in life we will always be.
Entwined our hearts will always be for eternity.

She loves me because I love with all my heart
As faithful forever I will truly be
Time will not change, whatever maybe
Cause we will always love each other to bits.

©J. A. Johnston
January 2006
Rev 12ᵗʰ July 2010

Remembrance

Wootten Bassett — Thank You: I was very touched by the scenes at Lyneham and Wootten Bassett during the repatriation of Service personnel during 2010, and wanted to say my personal 'thank you' to those who went to stand by the road in all weathers. Since writing this poem the town has received a Royal Warrant and is now known as Royal Wootten Bassett.

Grieving: When I thought of what I went through and how I behaved after I lost my first wife I was quite astounded. I wrote this poem to give others some comfort and hope.

Conscientious Objectors: I wrote this poem after hearing a rather biased discussion. Many 'Conscies' died doing good work; they just did not want to kill other humans.

Be Not Alone: This is another poem which I wrote to give comfort to those who have lost their loved one.

The Loss Felt: Watching a ceremony for the fallen on the television inspired the words in this poem.

Wootton Bassett – Thank You

Servicemen of Lyneham stand to attention on the runway
As a flagged draped coffin, in slow order, emerges the plane
Servicemen as pallbearers with tears but no shame.
They're honouring their fallen comrades - again.

The cortège drives through Wootton Bassett High Street
Lined by people, friends and family, several bodies deep,
Those not bereaved but feel the grief of those who have lost.
Flags of Regiments, Legions and others dipped in accost.

All those present showing their respect for those fallen.
For our brave lads and lassies fighting wars far away.
Costing young lives, families crying, carry such pain.
They all know that they will return here again.

Stand firm my friends let your hero's life not be in vain.
Be steadfast, firm and victory will be ours, through the pain.
To the people of Wootton Bassett a huge thanks to you.
For standing, in all weathers, to honour our youth.

©J. A. Johnston
10th November 2010
Painting by Carol Kibble

Remembrance:

Grieving

In life there are times of trial, times of sadness, times of gladness
At this time your life is in turmoil, or so it seems,
When you have lost a partner, dear friend or relative.
In this time of sadness, grieving is good and helps to heal the pain.

Do not look back with sadness in your heart
Do not despair, do not think; what if, why me?
Do not dwell on what might have been.
We must accept our loss, it is our lot.

Look forward to a new life ahead
Have your memories of the past instead.
Let those memories flow over you
But do not let them make you stew.

Life is for living and your future's ahead
They would not want you to grieve or be bitter
Only to remember with love and laughter
They want you, expect you, your life to regain.

"Their love will remain with you forever"

©J. A. Johnston
1st February 2008

Conscientious Objectors

Those who disagreed with war in the old days
Were called Conscies in a derisive way
White feathers were given to show others dismay
But most had a valuable part to play
In those terrible, our darkest, long gone days.

To carry arms, to fight, they would not care
Through principles that others could not share
To carry the wounded; oh yes they dared!
Their courage in this role cannot be denied
Many of those objectors, in war, did die.

In the mines: in ambulances: during the blitz
And to prisons some were confined; freedom deprived
Yet through it all they stood firm and tall
Their principles showing through with immense strength
But to others - seen as beneath their contempt.

First aid they rendered to our front line troops
Tramping through mud, dodging bullets, treating wounds
In no-man's land they often tramped in wet boots
Their courage must not be forgotten - so true
Those Conscies who would not fight for you.

So scorned they were by all around, so profound
But they steadfastly stood firm on principled ground.
Many forget the sacrifice these Conscies made
Died carrying the wounded to where treatment was found
Carrying the ones who scorned them out of hand.

©*J. A. Johnston*

5th October 2010

Remembrance:

Be Not Alone

Your life seems empty, your heart is heavy
The months and years ahead look bleak.
All seems lost, life seems very lonely.
Be not alone, be not afraid.

In this your hour of darkness, we are here.
Our support for you is beyond compare
Your friends are here, with a listening ear,
Be not alone, let us show we care.

Your time of need is shared indeed
By all that know you and some that don't,
They'll share your lot, they pray for your need.
Be not alone, share with us your grief.

Be not scared of those that do not understand,
Let them know that they are your friends.
They may not know your grieving hand.
They love you, they need you, be not alone.

©J. A. Johnston
24th July 2007

Remembrance:

The Loss Felt

All wars are fought to defend or gain
Leading to some people's greed, or pain.
Something that is not rightfully gained
Is not meant by God; but human brain.

When wars are done, lost lives counted.
There is no cure for the innocent's torment.
The loss felt by relatives or friends
Must be borne; with much sorrow and pain.

As time goes by and the pain is softened,
Families and friends ensure the lost are not forgotten.
Though the loss will always remain with them
The question of why; may never be explained.

©J. A. Johnston
12th September 2011

21

Making the Best of It

A Mind to Ponder: Witnessing how an unconscious patient was being moved around a hospital, on a stretcher, reminded me of my time as a patient. Whilst writing this poem I kept getting flashbacks of my time after I had a serious accident. I was able to use these memories to assist the forming of this poem.

Tomorrow Waits: This poem has proved to be the best I have written (so I'm told). It was originally composed to let my son know that I was thinking of him in his time of need. It has proven to be of use to others for all sorts of reasons.

Homeless and On the Streets: I think this poem explains itself.

Darkness in Life: A certain period in my life proved to be very difficult, made more difficult by those that put their own cast on the situation and as a result I was made to feel very lonely.

The Wheelchair: I wrote this after listening to a patient on an ambulance bitterly complaining about their lack of mobility. The patient was a perpetual moaner. I cannot claim that this poem made a difference BUT after the patient read it there was a change, for the better!

A Mind To Ponder

My eyes won't open I cannot see
I am shouting but no-one answers me
I'm moving my arms and legs in my mental agony
But no-one seems aware of my frustration but me.

If no-one hears what am I to do,
There is no pain but I cannot move,
Is anyone there to hear my scream.
I need some help! I need a wee.

There is a light I can see in the distance
So very bright it draws my eyes to its centre
But I have a fear that if I go there
I won't see my family again – ever.

The light is so strange as if it's guiding me
It's a very long way off; is this a dream
It would be so easy to follow that bright beam
But I keep hearing distant voices calling for me.

Slowly ever so slowly I start to regain
The feelings of my body and brain.
Firstly I hear but I can't answer my name.
Something is happening; I can feel pain.

PTO:

Making the best of it:

A Mind To Ponder: cont'd:

Very slowly my memory comes back
Memories like leaves in a storm, blown about
Not large enough for my memory to test
Making my brain giddy without a rest.

Slowly I surface to see faces peering at me
Someone says, 'Hello' I can't even squeak
I am aware that there are people and machinery.
I've been hurt; an accident it seems; not a dream.

©J. A. Johnston
20th June 20

Tomorrow waits

Today will have an ending,

Tomorrow starts anew,

Another chance to start again

When all your plans fall through.

Though sun may set on every dream

And toss to dust away,

Tomorrow's sun will rise again

To show this is your day.

This day will have an ending

Let trust in God be true

This day will pass and later;

Tomorrow waits for you.

©J. A. Johnston
February 2004

Making the most of it:

Homeless and on the Streets.

I sit here disconsolate in this gutter
Thinking not of my mother
But of the life I left behind
In the Children's Home; oh why!
Oh how could I be so blind?

I left the home at my own choice
All that food, bed and warmth
Left my friends in horrified disbelief
That I could leave them so easily.
The home had taught me pride - or conceit.

I now have no friends to call my own
Living under cardboard, that's my London town
Getting drenched when the rain comes down
Lose my possessions at the whim of a man.
My only shoes let my feet on the ground.

I walk all day and run when I have to
As gangs of boys want to beat me all blue
It's better to fight than to be a coward, true.
Run when a man tries to get in the bath tub
Escape to the darkness away from the hubbub.

The sunshine has warmth, my bones feel better
Boats on the Serpentine give me great pleasure.
My body is peeling from being so dirty
I must smell badly, my clothes are filthy.
The clothes that I wear are given by charity.

Homeless and on the streets cont'd:

I wake up early to avoid the do-gooders
Some say they'll help but have a hidden agenda.
All I want is to get off the streets
Be clean between lovely white sheets.
When will it happen for me to be normal?

I could have avoided this stressful existence.
All it needed was a call to the Home, for assistance,
But I had to prove I could cope on my own
If only someone had told me what it was, to be all alone.
I chose this way and the responsibility is mine, my own.

Was my honesty my downfall?
There were those who were kindly and good
And gave me leftovers that I was grateful for
They recognised I would not steal at all
But do a job or two for my food.

I cried myself to sleep many nights
With the cold and so many frights
Whilst all around seem in good cheer
I seem to live a life in continual fear.
I rue the day that I came here.

©J. A. Johnston
22ⁿᵈ January 2009

27

Making the best of it :

Darkness In Life

When life seems against us
And all appears lost, our mind in blackness
Our world is fragmented, our spirits are down
And those around us just do not understand.

There is no light at the end it seems
Life is worthless, no meaning or scheme
The blackness deepens and reason is lost
God has deserted us – what does this mean?

Through the darkness of our mind
Creeps unknown feelings – not understood
Others around you try to get through
Prayers are given – then not answered it seems.

Slowly but surely the light will shine
But help yourself – you must be bound
Those who love you are still around
Standing firmly – holding your ground.

J. A. Johnston
© February 1997

Making the most of it :

THE WHEELCHAIR

A problem with your hip or leg,
You should not be confined to bed,
Get up, get out and about, don't laze around,
You'll just get fat, we'll be bound.

But then they all hear you shout
"How the hell do I get out?
Here I am stuck at home
Mobility restricts me, I cannot roam".

'Ah ha' they then proclaim.
"We've a chariot with your name.
It has four wheels, a seat, a back,
A belt to stop you falling out,

They're even brakes to help you stop.
So off you go and try your luck".
Off down the street it's good to be out
Except the hills - which puff me out.

Now my mobility is much improved,
A wheelchair is my mode to move
Folded flat and in a car,
The worlds my oyster now I can roam far.

29

Prayers and Hymns

Do Not Forget: This a prayer that was written after I had visited someone and was thinking of how lucky I was to have a loving wife and secure home. I started to think of the Christmases I spent all alone and knowing that there are people out there who need our prayerful support.

Boy In A Stable: This was written as a result of my reading a letter from a friend who had just become a Christian and we had discussed why Jesus was still followed after 2010 years.

Battle Hymn: It was at the request of someone from Bath City Church who nagged me to write about fighting. I stated that I could not write poems at a request. An hour later I had written this poem and I gave him a copy. Later it became a hymn.

Rejoice: This was written because I wanted to sing something like a Salvationist hymn—i.e. bouncy!

Prayer - Church Re-opening: This prayer was written when the refurbishment of St Aldhelm's, Corsham was nearing completion.

Do Not Forget

Christmas cheer has now gone by
But think of those it passed on by
Those bereaved, injured or sick
Those out there, on their own, feeling the pits.
Think of those in a crowd, all alone
They have no friends to call their own.

Those so lonely, young and old
Are more so in the damp and cold
Their cries are silent, not heard at all
No one hears them; Oh, so alone!
Let them shiver, don't give a damn
Not my problem, my back's to them.

Relations, friends may be out there
If only they knew, would they care
Would they come to their aid
Give shelter, company, loving care
Resurrecting friendships lost to them
Offering hands of help with love, just being there.

So as the New Year enters in
Please remember those out there
Who are in need of love and care
Teach us all how to be there
To listen, to learn, to offer help to them
Those who are lonely now and then.

©*J. A. Johnston*
January 2005

Boy In A Stable

No room in the Inn was there that day
Only a stable with a manger, his head to lay
What a start for a baby that would one day
Be the Man who leads all the Christian way

If only they had known, would a bed have been found?
For a child who would one day, all confound?
By His learning and teachings at a very young age
Elders listened, as did the growing crowds.

With five loaves and fishes he fed the five thousand
What was left may have fed another thousand
And with water that he turned to wine
His followers grew, just like a vine.

Then He was persecuted and hung up to die
Nailed to a cross: baying crowds—oh how they cried!
Yet He forgave them in His agony
As He died, nailed, to a cross made from a tree.

In a world where He showed caring and love
They still nailed Him to a cross of wood
Why oh why did they do this to Him
All He wanted was for us to live without sin.

2011 years later He still lives on
In hearts, in words, written in song
When He rose again they all believed
Yes, He was the Son of God indeed.

©J. A. Johnston

Prayers and Hymns:

Battle Hymn

The battle of my life is not with You, O Lord
But against the ills of the human race.
The mental, physical, racial and religious.
The ills that show the sins of this world,
Even by those who say they believe in You.

Fight

The battle of my life is not with You, O Lord.
But against the ills I allow myself.
The deceitfulness, the thoughtlessness, and the anger,
The ills I allow take hold of me.
Even by those who appear to believe in You.

With

The battle of my life is not with You, O Lord.
But making myself acceptable to You.
By resolving my shallow indiscreet desires.
The ills of self I let engulf me.
Even by those who say they believe in You.

Faith

The battle of my life is not with You, O Lord.
But to confirm myself to be loved by You.
To show to all my true faith and love in my Lord,
Life gone by, left in the distant past.
Even by those who pray and believe in You.

To The

The victory of my life will be for You, O Lord.
To encourage others to believe and love You,
By showing my true faith and love of my Lord.
Past ills of my life, just that; well past.
I've joined all those who truly believe in You.

Cross

©J. A. Johnston
4th July 2010

33

CHRISTMAS

Dusk comes early,
This time of year,
As winter draws in,
And Christmas gets near.

The shops are a bustle,
People hurry by,
Money to spend,
Presents to buy.

Children full of glee,
Parents appease,
It's getting colder,
Don't you agree?

Dark clouds above,
As carols are sung
Snow may fall
'Wow' such fun!

Sing with good voice,
Songs of good cheer,
Our Saviour was born,
It's that time of year.

©*J. A. Johnston*
December 2004

Prayers and Hymns:

Rejoice

Rejoice; in the gift He has given you
If you will but open your eyes
Through Him you could have ever-lasting life
If you believe in Him.

Chorus:
If you now believe in Him (rpt)
His world is now open to you.
Rejoice, Rejoice, Rejoice

Rejoice; even though His life He gave
For you, yes you, and you alone.
Rejoice; He rose again from that grave
A better life to give you.

Chorus:

Believe in Him and He is yours
To fill your life with joy
Rejoice in Him, Rejoice in Him
A better life to live.

Chorus:

Amen

©J. A. Johnston
6th May 2010

Prayers and Hymns:

Prayer - Church Re-opening.

We give grateful thanks to you Lord for our Church.
For the Ministers and Elders that have led
worship to You in this church to date.
For all those that have worshipped here.
For all the works that have gone before us

As we use these refurbished premises
let us not forget we each have a part to play
in ensuring this opportunity for outreach is not wasted.
That all those who come, however trying,
are made to feel welcome in Your name.

We ask that You guide this church.
Ensure that we do not fail in our quest
To reach out to those who have not heard
or are in need of your name and peace.
Please ensure that we are not selfish with your gifts.

As we recommence our worship in this refreshed church
We thank you for all those who gave donations, however small,
that has enabled the work to be undertaken.
And, we hope, that in some small way, this work
Helped others to see witness for You.

©J. A. Johnston
21st November 2009

Christmas Poems

Christmas Joy: This was written during Christmas 2011 and forms the first of three poems celebrating the birth of our Lord.

A Baby Arrives. The second in the trilogy

Happy Birthday Jesus: Written at the suggestion of a dinner companion who felt people would pay more attention if a poem was written in this vein.

Christmas Wish: This was written when I was pondering the commercial aspects of Christmas and thinking of those who were on their own at this time.

Snowman III: It was fun watching some young people trying to make a snowman and I came to write this poem just for the fun of it.

Jesus' Birthday: The writing of this poem came about due to someone asking for a celebratory hymn. I had heard someone else say that no-one had written a birthday hymn for Jesus: so here it is.

Christmas: The writing of this poem took place whilst waiting for my wife as she shopped!

Christmas Joy

A baby arrived at Christmas
Of parents who were quite poor
He was to be a special boy
The whole world should adore.

As a boy He entered people's hearts
Telling of the way to heavenly paths
Speaking of His Father in terms of love
That we could share and live above.

They had no idea He was to become
The greatest thing since Rome
But even now 2000 years on
He's remembered in hearts, word and song

So once again as we celebrate
The birth of this special one
Christmas day is the birthday
Of God's gift to us – His Son.

©J. A. Johnston
17ᵗʰ December 2011

Christmas Joy

A baby arrived at Christmas
Of parents who were quite poor
He was to be a special boy
The whole world should adore.

As a boy He entered people's hearts
Telling of the way to heavenly paths
Speaking of His Father in terms of love
That we could share and live above.

They had no idea He was to become
The greatest thing since Rome
But even now 2000 years on
He's remembered in hearts, word and song

So once again as we celebrate
The birth of this special one
Christmas day is the birthday
Of God's gift to us – His Son.

©J. A. Johnston
17th December 2011

A Baby Arrives At Christmas

Jesus arrived on Christmas day,
To the sounds of animals eating hay.
No comfy bed for this little one
Only a manger for His head to lay.

Mary and Joseph, parents of Him
Could only find a stable at this Inn,
An unusual place for a child to be born
A child who one day would be king.

This child grew up as we all do
Except He was very special; true
Due to the miracles He did perform
Pharisees treated Him with scorn.

This child who grew to be a man
Came to earth by God's great hand
A gift to save us from our sins
Remember; Christmas is for Him.

Christmas Wish

Christmas is a happy time of year
Colourful, glittering, can bring a tear.

Money spent on presents to give.
People vying for the perfect gift.

Alas, there are those with nothing to spend
Are lonely, bereaved, homeless, no friend?

God gave His Son at this time
To show how we should be kind.

Like the three wise men of old
Who gave gifts to a child; so bold.

He showed how to treat the lonely and poor
So, take time out, spare a thought

For all those less fortunate; and those that pine.
Just like Christ did during His lifetime.

Snowman III

I stand not moving at all
Round and fat, not very tall
I have a hat upon my head
A scarf wrapped around my neck.

Two lumps of coal serve for eyes.
With a big orange carrot for a nose.
A mouth so wide I seem to smile.
A coat, unfilled arms, it is not mine.

The coat reaches down to the ground.
I have no feet on which to stand.
I cannot turn my head around
Or move away from where I stand.

I stand here watching the world pass by.
Children; apples of their parents' eye
Give cuddles and even a kiss.
If life remained like this; Oh bliss.

Christmas Poems:

Snowman III cont'd:

Alas, although the children had such fun
I will disappear with the sun.
But have no fear, I'll be back next year,
If the snow falls and children are here.

As I melt into the ground on which I stand
Do not mourn my passing on,
I am pleased you've had such fun
But like the winter, life moves on.

©J. A. Johnston
20ᵗʰ November 2008

42

Christmas Poems:

Jesus' Birthday

Jesus was born of Mary
At Christmas time of the year.
Born in Bethlehem, Judea
2000 plus years ago

Chorus:　　　*Christ was born at Christmas time*
Let's celebrate each year
with music, readings and hymns
Giving special praises to Him.

A manger was his cradle
As there was no room at the Inn
Animals gave Him warmth
As people travelled to Him

Chorus:

Remembering His lowly birth
He achieved most marvelous things
Because He is the Son of God
A Saviour who is our King.

Chorus

For those that are unbelievers
Remember He died along ago
Yet He is still worshiped
In hearts, minds, and song.

Animal Antics

The Fox Cubs:: I was sitting in Sidney Gardens, Bath one pleasant evening. Suddenly two fox cubs appeared and the rest is in the poem.

Little Thrush: Sitting in Henrietta Park, Bath this little bird kept hopping and skipping about as if asking for food. Read what happened next..

The Mouse: Do you have a cat, or two Don't they just love to bring you presents. This is what happened with one of the cats presents.

The Music of the Birds: I love to sit in parks as the summer evenings close in and the birds are singing their songs. I find it very relaxing and it encourages me to write.

2 Cats and 1 Dog: I wrote this poem at 7am this morning (9th Jan 2012) as I found I was short of poems for the completion of 'Animal Antics'. The inspiration was from Jessie my sons cat, who is now 18 years old, a grand old lady.

The Fox Cubs

Whilst I sit here breathing in the air
A pair of fox cubs suddenly appear
Playing with the leaves on the ground
Gambolling across the grass and sand
They're having such great fun!
They seem oblivious to me sitting in the sun
Watching as they enjoy the air
Keeping an eye on their lair.

Little Thrush

A Thrush, it skips and hops about
Flitting and flying around and about.
Pecking here and there seeking a worm for supper.
Getting ever nearer to me
Hoping for a tit-bit, it seems.

It flies off a meter or two
Then skips back "I'm looking at you"
I feel obliged and break off some bread
He flew away: I think it was "thanks" he said.

The little Thrush comes back for more
Chasing off others that want his store.
"What's that? - A cat – oops!, I'm out of here"
The Thrush quickly flies away - later to re-appear..

©J. A. Johnston
July 2006
Picture by A. Curry

The Mouse

A little snout appeared from round the chair
I knew it was a snout because it had sparse pointed hair.
It was wet upon the nose but didn't dribble I suppose
BUT the eyes they were so very curious, roaming side to side
Whiskers some may call them but they were sticking out a treat
As it looked at me, oh, so, very sort of sweet!
It stared so very hard at me and wondered 'what is it that I can see?
It is much bigger than the cat that brought me here
But it is not moving, is it something I should fear'?
The mouse crept further out, showed his body from tail to snout
Then a rustle I did hear as Jessie suddenly appeared
'Gotcha' the cat seemed to say, as she pounced,
grabbed the mouse, and ran out through the door.
I ran as fast I could and beat the cat to the back door
And mouse now enjoys its freedom once more.

©J. A. Johnston
25th November 2007

47

Animal Antics:

The Music of The Birds

The music of the birds up in the trees
Give background noise as the sun shines on me
The day is balmy with clear blue sky
The sound of trains rolling by.

The sound of the trains rolling by
Draws my attention to passers-by
Walking their dogs or children without leads
Making merry in the garden of Sidney.

Making merry in the garden of Sidney
I'm left to dream in my imagine
Thinking of a wonderful wife
Listening to birds making music – what a life

©J. A. Johnston
24th June 2008

2 Cats & 1 Dog

Little grey whiskers appeared through the door
Followed by a head and body with silver grey paws
Willow has arrived with a 'yowl' of delight
To see if there's food to satisfy her diet.

Very soon the cat flap clatters once again
This time a black cat, as if on a chain.
On seeing young Willow Jessie sidles by
As Willow fizzes and gives a warning cry.

The sound of foot pads heard on the stairs
Then suddenly our dog Scampi appears and stares
'What's all the fuss he seems to be saying
But Willow and Jesse just, completely ignore him.

Two cats and a dog make for interesting times
Their antics can be quite entertaining in the least
With Willow chasing Scampi up the stairs, at speed
Jessie is looking quite, well, displeased.

The cats bring presents for members of the family
We need to be careful that Scampi does not eat.
Though Willow and Scampi have now passed on
With Jessie we can remember such great fun.

Fun Time:

Ooh La La!: I was asked to provide some poems for a fund raising book for our Church. I wrote this whilst sitting in a café watching the world go by and observing what people bought. I thought this ideal for a book that had recipes as well as poems.

Puddings: Another poem for the fund raising book which has since drawn a lot of comments during presentations.

Dad Your Parkinson's A Pain: When I discovered I had Parkinson's I was upset but my natural instinct was to 'take the rise' so looking on the bright side I came up with this poem.

A Good Night's Sleep: This poem was the result of thinking about us 'old-uns' getting ready for bed! NOT especially myself.

Laughing Child: I wrote this after watching some young children at play in a church coffee morning.

Ooh La La!

Tall dark rich and handsome
Makes a girl want to meet 'um
Caught my eye – can't be shy
Could be the apple of my eye!
Looking, oh so lovely and dreamy
Being full and oh so creamy
Makes me think of being naughty
But what if Grandma caught me?

Oh I just can't wait!
Oh what a fuss I would make!
Even if I do put on a little weight
If I could, just have a little, well some
Of that scrumptious looking chocolate cake!

8ᵗʰ June 2008

Puddings

What sort of pudding do you like?
Is it suet with jam or spice?

Would you prefer a proper steam duff
Jam roly-poly like mother used to love!

Is your apple pie served with custard or cream
Or perhaps a pie full of glorious gooseberries!

Like my wife would you like crème-bruelie
Perhaps a bowl of strawberries, or a sundae.

Bananas and custard are a favourite dish
Chocolate mud pie with lovely whipped cream.

Thick rice pudding with egg custard on top
My lips are drooling as I write about this lot.

Perhaps a gateaux covered in fruit sauce; Apricot?
Fresh fruit salad with ideal milk – and cream!

Would any of these be your pudding dream?

©*J. A. Johnston*
8th June 2008

Fun Time:

"Dad Your Parkinson's A Pain"

My Dad's got Parkinson's
But he can be quite useful
His hand can shake quite violently
But he knows a few tricks to pull.

When dinner time comes round
And Mum wants the gravy mixed
She just gives Dad the bowl
And he hangs grimly to his whisk.
It's mixed smoothly in a jiff

When at the urinal he stands
Watch out when he has shaking hand-
He has such a sheepish grin
As he comes out of the loo -
Well he did just wash his hands, true!

If my daughter needs to have a nap
I put her in Dads loving arms
It's not long before his shakes
Sends her to dreamy lands.

He tried to paint her bedroom
Did he do it well? – Not on your nell
It looked like it had rained inside
Our Mother gave him hell.

I guess there are 'worse things in life'
As Dad is wont to say
But I do wish he would not stay
So cheerful, useful and kind
Then I could have a moan and say
"Dad your Parkinson's a pain"

©J. A. Johnston
11th January 2011

53

A Good night's Sleep

Visit the loo and have a wee
This will make you very comfy
Put your teeth into a glass
Slip into bed and relax at last
Pick-up your book or turn on the telly
It's not yet time to lie on your belly.

As your partner slides in beside you
Make sure there's space - or woe betide you.
Blow your nose and clear your passages.
Put down your book, turn off the telly.
Puff up your pillows, take your pills.
Turn out the light oops; kiss your partner goodnight.

Fun time:

Laughing Child

Little child enjoying his time
Having a laugh all the while
As his father plays a game
Little child giggling all the same.

Little child enjoying her time
Plays with dolls as if a child
Helps mum make cakes, or a mess
Little girl laughing at mum's distress.

Young man now at his father,s height
Working with Dad or enjoying his sport
Young ladies he looks at with a little gleam
Hoping to meet one who will be his queen.

Young lady now shapely as to the boys
Has forgotten her dolls and toys
Acts all coy and crestfallen too
Especially when the boy refuses to coo.

They're both fully grown, the nest they have flown
They both have partners to call their own
It won't be long before the cycle begins
When families they make, l hope it's not twins!

©J. A. Johnston
22nd October 2006

Mobility

A Chariot: I wrote this poem just for the fun of it after watching Tammy Grey on the TV. What an inspiration she is to chair bound people.

A Bike for a Girl: This poem was written whilst I was a volunteer with 'Bikes 4 Africa' (a very worth while charity). I was struck by the way the girls in Africa took to leaning how to ride their bikes. Falling off seemed to be 'par for the course' rather than feeling the hurt caused by the fall.

The Motor Car: I wrote this poem back in the distant days of 1982. I was working on the Railway Enquiries desk and wrote this between calls. Just a bit of fun really!

Our Journey: This poem was written much later. It tells about our journey to and with our Lord.

The Trip: Filling in time whilst waiting for a train this poem came to mind and I wrote it in about 15minutes.

Mobility:

A Chariot

I have four wheels, padded seat and back.

Some brakes to stop me rolling down the slightest shap.

A seatbelt to stop one from falling out.

I trundle along all sedate and prim

Unless I get stuck , or my wheels in the mud spin.

Maybe pushed or self propelled

Dependant on required or available willing help.

I have three wheels and a long snout

I cause a lot of people to scream and shout.

I'm long and thin and speed's my thing

I race around a big race track.

Tammy Gray once champion of the world pack

Now retired, handed over to Jack?

Or some other person whose good on the track.

I am made for the sick and lame

It gives them freedom to roam ere their game

Shops with wide aisles allow browsing again.

I come in all shapes and sizes so disabled gain.

I give freedom to those with bad knees, back or hip pain

Who would otherwise be confined to home with no trips

I am made for them a wheelchair, a chariot.

©J. A. Johnston

Mobility:

A Bike For A Girl

A girl on her bike laughs with delight
As she falls off onto the dusty road
She does not care the scraped elbows and knees
Because to her a bike is heaven sent; a need.

As she climbs back aboard, rides a little more
Then falls off in gales of glee.
For she knows that soon she'll ride to school
And not have to walk dusty streets.

When she's mastered the art of riding her bike
She'll find it easier to improve her writing
'Cause she'll not be so tired or exhausted
When at school she'll be early arriving.

Her family will be pleased; regardless of scrapped knees
As she'll be less tired when she gets home
As less tired she is; the more she'll achieve
Making her family extremely well pleased.

6th June 2010

The Motor Car

The motor car was built by man
For man's convenience
In comfort, style and elegance
He travels o're there in.

Black, blue, greens and reds
Two tones some think blest
But Saturdays their polishing
To make theirs shine the best.

Colours are important
For everyone can see
A bit of personality
In these elegant machines.

They speed along the man built roads
On journeys too and fro'
To work, on holiday
And only heaven knows.

They shine, they gleam
Whenever clean, but rust
Away as well, and sadly finish
On the heap, when their life is done.

J. A. Johnston
©October 1982

59

Mobility:

Our Journey

Help us start our journey to You O Lord
A journey that is long and rough.
We must bear our tribulations
So that we might respect our obligations.

As we travel along Your road
Make us look for You to behold
Show a light that we may
In Your love strengthen and grow.

When we have found You O Lord
Walk with us along the way
Take our hand and lead us on
Through this world to the Promised Land.

©J. A. Johnston
5th December 2010

Mobility:

The Trip

The sun is shinning, the day is bright
Flowers, colours of every hue, blossom all around
Streets are filled with shoppers out walking
Children crying, running and laughing
Parents frustrated at every turning
By children just not listening.

Vehicles flowing too and fro
Down the streets they do go.
Traffic lights regulating flow
Into coffee shops, wimpy bars to feed
To drink and converse to indulge
All these people going their own way
Carrying out life's great play.

People travel further a-field
By car, train and bus
Long journeys to enjoy
Destinations each one agreed
To family, friends whatever appeals
May even a shopping spree appeal
But on their way they do travel
Hoping their trip will be beneficial.

©J. A. Johnston
June 2006

Out and About

Bath: Walking through the back streets of Bath one day, I spotted an advert for entries of art and poetry for a competition. The subject was Bath. I was sat in Parade Gardens when these words came to me. I have not found that shop since so the poem never got into the competition. Never mind—aye!

The Village: Enjoying a walk through Steeple Ashton one day, I was struck by the beauty of the place and was inspired to write this poem some time later.

Corsham Town: This poem was written as an experiment. Could I write a poem on a specific subject, at the request of someone? Did it work? Only you can tell.

Tranquil Place: I was sitting in a park one evening when I wrote this. It was so quiet and peaceful that I thought I could hear God talking to me.

Café Church: I was so impressed with Café Church in Yatton Keynell that I was inspired I write this poem as a tribute to Wanda, Lynn, Morag and Annie not forgetting the others that assist the running of the coffee mornings.

Out and About:

Bath

Chimneys standing on the roof so tall,
On top of houses built in days of yore.
Victorians and Edwardians have left their mark
In their buildings and beautiful parks

Woods, old and younger, built Bath in stone
Whilst Beau Nash made socialites his own.
Bath's history has a story to tell
From Roman days thru' two thousand and ten.

There's a museum with the name Holburne
Lots of art for the discerning person to learn.
In The Passage is a very old gateway,
Harping back to the Romans hey-day.

The Abbey is resplendent in the sun or rain
Its beautiful bells ring out a hymn each day.
Many nations come to this 'World Heritage' city.
The Romans came, and left, - what a pity.

Famous for its hot baths and min'ral waters.
I am pleased to be one of many authors
Inspired by Bath's tranquil atmosphere
It's so easy to write poems and stories here.

©J. A. Johnston.
9th September 2008

Out and About:

The Village

I stroll along a country lane with hedgerows either side,
Greens and yellows of every hue line my walk with splendour.
Wild flowers of a wide variety with bushes even wilder.
I listen to the wildlife sounds as down the lane I wander
Birds wild cacophony make, at my passing, as young ones they protect.

I find myself so enthralled, unnoticed into a village I have strolled.
Walking along the village lane I look at large houses with roofs of thatch
The sunlight on the windows twinkling; no smoke from stacks.
Seeing over a wall I spy a lady gardening, a child on a swing playing.
Beautiful flowers the lady is attending, trim lawns descending.

A pleasant 'Good morning' we exchange as I pass along the way
To see lovely thatched cottages and a manor house still standing.
I spy a village pub – the 'Toby' by it's naming
The landlady is welcoming and pleasant so I have a pint and pie.
We gossip, as I drink and eat, about the local area, time passes by.

I wend my way along the village lanes, pass the green, quiet this day
Imagining cricket, being played; the sound of leather on willow
As in my mind I hear the shouts as spectators give encouragement,
What a splendid picture it would make on a lovely summer day.
But I must carry on my way if I am to reach my home today.

©J. A. Johnston
13th November 2007

64

Out and About:

Corsham Town

I hear a screech that makes me jump and turn around
Then I spy a feathered display, what a beauty.
The colours of the rainbow, head topped with a crown.
This bird, a Peacock, has the run of Corsham Town.

I continue my walk through an avenue of trees
A lovely walk through Corsham Court, there's a light breeze.
The autumn greens and gold's, the colours of the leaves.
Such beauty is from the hand of God, I do believe.

Along the road to the Alms Houses, such pretty architecture,
The history of Corsham, shown in such great splendour.
The old school room from the 1668 is still here
School children shown, an insight into the past, without fear.

St Bartholomew's, stands with graves from days of long ago.
The walls stand tall and strong, roof vaults high and arched.
The sound of voices in song, are ethereal in their sound
I cannot but be moved by the ambiance that is found.

I view weavers' cottages, from a trade of times gone by.
I stroll past cafes, pubs, independent shops where you can buy,
Or sample the history that makes this town so sublime.
It's why my family chose Corsham in which to reside.

©J. A. Johnston
3rd November 2008

Out and About:

Tranquil Place

The quietness of this lovely place
Helps with my mind to rest
Away from the bustle of life's fast pace
Sitting, relaxing in this tranquil place

If He is there for me to speak
Then possibly I will heavens peace receive
For through the years I have not listened
Perhaps this place is at last for Him.

The background noises mildly effect
The quiet tranquil setting of this restful place
Sounds of canal boats, trains and people
Not infringing on this beautiful setting.

As I sit here enjoying my rest
Quietly enjoying the still atmosphere
Knowing that a spirit is near
Talking to me if only I will hear.

©J. A. Johnston
17 October 2005

Café Church

Café Church is such a treat
A place for villagers to meet
The open door means others may greet
And all may have a Christian treat.

Café Church has such wonderful cakes
Made by villagers, free contribution they make
Such a lovely old church and atmosphere
Means villagers chat and listen here.

Café Church is very real socialising
All who come will feel they are drawn in
To this very special social gathering
Enjoying the village and church interacting.

Café Church is staffed by lovely people
There to help greet and feed you
A warm welcoming atmosphere prevails
In Café Church they share Christian values.

©J. A. Johnston
20ᵗʰ August 2007

Finally

Stand Tall and Proud: I wrote this poem as a favour to a nurse whilst in hospital. Nurse wanted a poem similar to 'A Friend' but reflecting their religious beliefs. Once again the person was very pleased with the end result, although it took about 15 minutes to write.

A Friend : Once again I was asked to write a poem by someone for a sick relative. I was in the Art Café in Melksham at the time. This poem appeared 10 minutes after I had stated I would go away and see what I could write. She was vey pleased.

Love Is Yours: This was written on the spur of the moment whilst thinking of Valentines day. You have to write when it is in your head or lose it. Love is all around us and not just for today.

Our Journney: I wrote this, during a service, reflecting on my own situation in relation to my service to the community.

A Nation True; This was written to encourage others to take pride in Great Britain after I listened to a programme on the television about the lack of commitment by British people to this fair isle.

Finally:

Stand Tall and Proud

You both stand tall and proud in God's sight
My best friends in this part of my life.
To me and others that I have known
Nothing is too much; you keep me right
On God's path even in darkest night.

You both, by example, prove that love is free
For those who care to accept Jehovah's
Unconditional, uncomplicated love.
Given without seeking any reward.
Just give a little devotion to our Lord.

If I would have my life over again
You are the ones I would seek to retain
As you are uncomplicated friends,
Who seek no personal gain,
In helping others to reach their aims.

In helping others you make no claims.
Quietly working in your friendly way
Through their mist; in God's name.
Gently coaxing them down life's path
With commonsense, affection and love.

©J. A. Johnston
8ᵗʰ November 2011

Finally:

A Friend

A friend is a person who knows me well
To whom all my troubles I can tell.
A person that will not me persuade
That I should do things their way.
A listening ear when there is a need
Always there with no sign of greed.
A laugh and a giggle to share together.
To go for walks in all kinds of weather.
To share my life when all said and done
A friend such as you is a blessing for one.
A person in my life I am glad to have won.

©J. A. Johnston
10ᵗʰ March 2011

Finally:

Love is Yours

I feel I am writing something very contrite
When I write, or say, I love you, both day and night
But oh my love you see it's true
All I ever wanted was to be with you.

I hope in the progress of years and days
Our bond will get stronger and never fray
As through life's journeys we travel on our way
And we learn more of each other as together we stay.

©J. A. Johnston
10th February 2008

Our Journey

Help us start our journey to You O Lord
A journey that is long and rough.
We must bear our tribulations
So that we might respect our obligations.

As we travel along Your road
Make us look for You to behold
Show a light that we may
In Your love strengthen and grow.

When we have found You O Lord
Walk with us along the way
Take our hand and lead us on
Through this world to the Promised Land.